# PoetFlow Anthology

Curated by
Christina Miller
& Vince Font

Published by Glass Spider Publishing
www.glassspiderpublishing.com
ISBN 9781798422731
Library of Congress Control Number: 2019939716
Cover photo by Sarah Cox
Photo page 39 by Rachelle Greenwell
Photo page 47 by Christina Miller
Photos page 53, 55 by Cindy Jones
Photo page 73 by Jayrod Garrett
Edited by Vince Font

GLASS**SPIDER**PUBLISHING

# Introduction

Janica Johnstun moved from Texas to Ogden, Utah, in September of 2015. Being new to town with no support system, she created PoetFlow as an outlet to connect with others and to express hope through creative artistry. The Lighthouse Lounge was there to support Janica and provide a home to PoetFlow. That first PoetFlow open mic was led by Janica and attended by Christina Miller and Kase Johnstun. Over the past three years, PoetFlow has continued to grow and has become a family of support for those who regularly attend.

PoetFlow was created to provide a safe space for local poets and writers to share their words. Through the sharing and baring of souls through spoken word, the members of PoetFlow have grown together as a supportive community, endearing the weaving of our life stories together.

Every writer is embraced at PoetFlow, from amateur poets to published writers. We are about community as much as we are about creative artistry. All are welcome to visit, listen, and share at the open mic each week at the Lighthouse Lounge. The poetry featured here is from our PoetFlow community, including regular members and guest poets.

# Odes to PoetFlow

# PoetFlow

Sarah Cox

I started coming to support a good friend. I figured one time and that would be the end.

Two years later and here I still am. Surrounded by the best of new-found friends.

I know all of your stories, and you know mine, too. My deepest, darkest secrets, that I only tell you.

I've always loved words, but was more of just a talker. You nerds taught me to write out my feelings and the fact that that worked was a real fucking shocker!

I've laughed and I've cried. Gave hugs and high fives. I look forward to Tuesdays, they fill my heart full. I love coming to PoetFlow, and that is no bull.

So what has PoetFlow meant to me? I can't quite put it into words. But one thing I know is: I love all you nerds!

# PoetFlow

Leonides Ortiz

As waves crash over me, I fight to stay up
But the waves keep coming;

Waves of doubt
Waves of worry
Waves of loneliness and rejection
Waves of fear
Waves upon waves upon waves

Battering me like a rag doll
Left then right then left again

I lose all sense of direction except for down
And…
Down I go – I am so tired I can't fight the waves

As I slowly sink I see prisms of light scattering all across
Like the night sky full of stars

I begin a nocturnal fall; the permanent sleep

Splash-----

My view is interrupted and I jolt awake
My body surges to the surface and it breaks like shattered
glass
I grab hold of the life saver and I inhale greedily—I've been
starving

Looking around I see in the distance the scattering of
lighthouses along the shore
instilling the calmness, I sought for so long

You, my dear friends, my chosen family, are the lighthouses
Your words reverberate through the mic and bounce off the
walls like beacons of light
I will always look for those beacons of light

You have been my saviors and when I see the beacons,
I know I am safe; I know I am home

I am forever grateful that you save me
You save me every week.

# Untitled

Mary Luna

I fell on my way to PoetFlow.
My hand broke my fall.
This time, this fall, I caught myself on my own.
I could get up, so I did.

A young man saw me fall and called out, "oh no!"
But he offered no help (and none was requested).
Because this time, this fall, I got up on my own.
He moved on.

I moved on, crossing the street.
No second guessing, no over-thinking.
I simply got myself up and moved on.

This woman is steady;
this one who catches herself,
who moves on.

Every time, every fall, getting up on her own.

Part II
No falls on the way home from PoetFlow.
My arm linked with theirs.
This time, this path, I asked not to be alone.
I could embrace and trust, so I did.

My friend called out in laughter.
Help wanted. Reciprocated.
This time, these friends, no desire to be on my own.

We walked on, crossing the street.
Entangled in trust, filled with happiness,
We simply kept up and lived on.

This tribe is strong;
These ones who love and support.

This time, this joy, connected in Love.

# What PoetFlow Means to Me

Rachelle Greenwell

The end of a season all the leaves had dropped from my tree. I was left barren. Empty and cold. One day Sarah messaged me and said let's go to PoetFlow. I was nervous my self-esteem had taken a huge blow. New situations always make me anxious. "Can I wear my Spiderman shirt" I asked. "You can totes wear your Spiderman shirt," she replied.

I came that first time for two reasons, to get out of my house that had become so painful to live in and to listen to poetry, which is one thing I have always loved.

I remember Janica reading a poem. Within that poem was a line that completely hit home to me. It echoed my own thoughts but with words I hadn't thought to use to describe them. I don't remember the line. But i do remember nervously approaching her after to have her repeat it. She welcomed me with such grace.

Week after week I came. I listened and felt welcome. I met Jayrod and his booming voice. Christina and her clever writing.

I came to the realization that the group is not about sharing great works, although great works are shared. I learned that no one was criticizing and that every genre of writing was acceptable. So I got up some courage and read some pieces that I'd written long ago. Back when writing was a huge part of my life.

The first time at the mic I was very scared, but felt very supported.

Over a time I watched writers come to the mic and speak about times that had crushed their souls. Experiences that had changed their lives. They shared very personal thoughts.

I watched them leave the mic to applause and embraces. No judgment in sight. After living in a lifetime of judgement this felt like sunshine to me. Week after week I saw how a burden would be removed and their aura completely change after reading. I knew that was something I desperately needed.

So even though I had gone just to listen I began to write. I wrote of my darkest times. Putting into words what I felt and remembered. I watched the words drop onto paper. Some logical and some nonsensical. Emotions that had been stored in my psyche for so long come dripping out onto the page through my hand.

Even though I wrote I didn't feel the burdens lifted like I saw in my friends. I realized the final stage was to read out loud. It seems we absorb each other's experiences in this group making it easier for all of us to carry them. The Lighthouse is a sacred space. Where we can leave our burdens at each other's feet and they won't be trodden on, but handled with care and sent on their way. We are a special tribe, a family all with our own strengths to add to the stew. I don't know what kind of person I would be without this group. I do know I'd still be living in the darkness and misery that encumbered my soul. I am so grateful to all of you.

# Guest Poets

We are grateful to the following poets, all of whom have shared works to be reprinted in this book:

Brad Roghaar
Shanielle Faith
Shanan Ballam
Star Coulbrooke
Allison McLennan

# How Geese Fly

Brad Roghaar

In the Yellowstone, in the winter,
right where the Lewis River meets
the head water of the Snake,
there is an oasis—a nut-brown island
surrounded by diamond white snow and
covered with the droppings of geese.

Warmed by hot springs, in the cold of winter,
this particular spot of ground
never gives to snow, the flakes harmless
where they land,
sucked into the soil like vapor.

Here is sanctuary, a full acre of warmth—
a full acre of geese.

If you should find yourself there—
run fast toward the confluence.
Your arms will want to rise at the shoulder
and rapidly fall to your sides.

You need not scream.
As you run, the geese (all thousand of them)
will begin (in a great slow rush)
to fly—a chaos without proportion.

You will see that they gain height,
painfully slow.

You may be struck hard by the sight
of those ridiculously outstretched necks
(the diameter of a child's wrist),
vulnerable
so far ahead of their beating source of power.

And as those necks appear to pull
that awkward body into the air,
you will note those wild eyes straining
black and backward—all panic, terror of
impossibility.

But you will also note that geese never
miss their takeoff. You will note that
                    they never crash.

You will see
(in the deafening sound of this great
honking and beating of air)
that all of this will work.

You will know the unity of chaos.

And this is the miracle
that you will witness
in the Yellowstone, in the winter,
on a simple island of geese droppings
where the Lewis meets the Snake.

# Home

Shanielle Faith

He said, "I'm so full,
I feel as big as a house."
I said, "If you were a house,
I'd live inside of you."
which is to say
I'd decorate your insides
with all of the finest paintings.

I would stroke your walls with my
fingertips slowly feeling you out,
finding where the cracks are
and where the plaster's chipped
then just letting it be that way.

If you were a house,
you'd be a fixer-upper
which is to say I'm no carpenter,
but I'm woman enough to adore
you for all of your charm,
willing to recognize beauty in
what others may see as flaws,
and believe me when I say
you don't have to fix a thing.

I love your electrical problems.
Not every light knows exactly
the right time to provide the perfect
amount of spark,
and that's okay.

I love your dodgy plumbing
always spraying me soaking wet
at the most unexpected times.
It keeps things exciting.
At least your foundation
isn't crumbling. At least you're already
everything you need to be.

If you were a house,
you'd have a skylight.
I'd lie beneath your ceiling
and peer up at the constellations
through your window,
roll around on the floor of your
living room that is also your heart,
and laugh alone inside of it.

If you were a house,
you would be so full,
but I'm not talkin' awkward, old
pictures from the past and
ugly furniture in the attic, full.
I'm talkin' sunlight through windows.
I mean breakfast on the stove
and coffee when it's cold,
full of all of the important things.
Like love.

Because even if you think yourself a house,
the truth is, you've always been home,
and I want to make my place in you.

# The Girl

Shanielle Faith

I ask Ogden if I can come over
for the night. She says she
always leaves her doors
unlocked for me.
I'd be lying if I said I didn't
get my mouth up in her sometimes.
I'd also be lying if I said she didn't like it.
At least, I think she likes it.

She's the kind of girl
who has a Lighthouse inside of her.
It shines from her eyes as if to say
there's no last call.
She's never closing,
and she never pretends to be anything
she's not.

My mother is Salt Lake City,
and she's only clean on the outside
to hide how dirty she is on the inside.
I think that's why I like Ogden so much.
She knows who she is
and isn't always trying to clean up her house
or her heart for the strangers who might visit.
She knows no one is eyeing her as closely
as she eyes herself
which means she's never asking me
to wipe my feet at the door.
She knows we all got shit on our shoes.

And deep down, she loves herself.
I tell her I love her, too, while
we're both naked.
She smiles with a wink and
tells me I'm cute.

# Obituary Addendum #1: Survived by Father

Shanan Ballam

Dylan Alexander Thomas
April 20, 1989-July 7, 2013

~~Syracuse, Utah—Dylan passed away on Sunday, July 7th, 2013.~~
~~He was born on April 20, 1989 in Ogden Utah to David and Sally Thomas. He was the youngest of five children.~~
~~Dylan lived the first several years of his life in~~ [Nordic Valley, Utah] ~~before living in such places as South Ogden; North Ogden; Servern, Maryland; Logan, Utah; and Albuquerque, New Mexico.~~
~~He lived in Syracuse, Utah for the past several years of his life. He was employed by Wal-Mart and Little Caesar's Pizza.~~
~~Dylan was a musical genius, with guitar being his passion. He slept with his guitar every night. He was good-natured, funny, quirky, and loved by all who knew him. Many people who knew Dylan considered him to be their baby brother.~~
~~He is~~ [survived by father,] ~~David L. Thomas; mother, Sally Perry Thomas; siblings Shanan (David) Ballam; Marcy Gross; Alyson (Troy) Frederick; Sean Thomas; nephews Jeremiah Peterson and Jayden Peterson; niece Alyvia Chavez; stepmother, Misty Thomas.~~
~~He was preceded in death by his grandparents, Wilmer "Bud" Perry and Fay Thomas Perry, his cousin Daniel Perry, and his brother Aiden Thomas.~~
~~Dylan, we love you so much. We miss you terribly. We will never forget you. Rock on forever, little brother.~~

Dylan Alexander Thomas
April 20, 1989-July 7, 2013
*Obituary Addendum #1: Survived by Father*

Nordic Valley, Utah—The rest of us kids Dad called
*worthless*, *chickenshit*, and we crept around the cold house,
dissolved ourselves into shadow, trying, always, to dodge
dad's brain-shrieking slaps to the backs of our heads. Dylan
burst into the world, eyes adjusting to dad's drunk and
stumbling danger, 'til Dylan's eyes smoldered a secret anger
all his own, and soon he grew wild brown curls that even at
three he refused to get cut. One afternoon, in the gray living
room, Dyl danced around in his bright green ninja turtle t-
shirt, diaper off. I told him to apologize to dad for refusing
his diaper. He waved his little dick at dad taunting *I'm sorry
dad, I'm sooooo sorry dad!* I cringed—my skin pricked cold
knowing the red, ruthless strike—*Stop, Dylan, stop!* I begged,
but he wouldn't. There he was, three-years-old, calling dad
out, calling him on—*Fuck You!* said Dyl's little dick flapping
up and down. Dad's face changed dangerous, black rising in
his eyes. Then he threw back his head—I could see all his
teeth—and he laughed 'til his voice rasped. My father
laughed so hard he cried.

# Obituary Addendum #2: Minor in Possession

Shanan Ballam

Dylan Alexander Thomas
April 20, 1989-July 7, 2013

~~Syracuse, Utah—Dylan passed away on Sunday, July 7th, 2013.~~
~~He was born on April 20, 1989 in Ogden Utah to David and Sally Thomas. He was the youngest of five children.~~
~~Dylan lived the first several years of his life in Nordic Valley, Utah before living in such places as South Ogden; North Ogden; Servern, Maryland;~~ [Logan, Utah;] ~~and Albuquerque, New Mexico.~~
~~He lived in Syracuse, Utah for the past several years of his life. He was employed by Wal-Mart and Little Caesar's Pizza.~~
~~Dylan was a musical genius, with guitar being his passion. He slept with his guitar every night. He was good-natured, funny, quirky, and loved by all who knew him. Many people who knew Dylan considered him to be their baby brother.~~
~~He is survived by father, David L. Thomas; mother, Sally Perry Thomas; siblings Shanan (David) Ballam; Marcy Gross; Alyson (Troy) Frederick; Sean Thomas; nephews Jeremiah Peterson and Jayden Peterson; niece Alyvia Chavez; stepmother, Misty Thomas.~~
~~He was preceded in death by his grandparents, Wilmer "Bud" Perry and Fay Thomas Perry, his cousin Daniel Perry, and his brother Aiden Thomas.~~
~~Dylan, we love you so much. We miss you terribly. We will never forget you.~~ [Rock on forever, little brother.]

Dylan Alexander Thomas
April 20, 1989-July 7, 2013
*Obituary Addendum #2: Minor in Possession*

Logan, Utah—Midnight, you stood in handcuffs in the
driveway while the house thudded and glowed with the
post-wedding party. The cop was friendly, pleased at your
etiquette, and he was terribly sorry but he'd still have to
charge you with minor in possession. "I get it, man. You
have to do your job" you said. The cop asked "where'd you
get the beer?" You replied "I totally stole it" and winked at
me. My legs almost collapsed—this was my ass on the line—
but I know you never cracked under pressure, Dylan. Never.
The officer, smiling, released you into my custody, and the
whole house celebrated your vindication: Tall Chris poured
wine from a silver bag down all our throats, Jack Daniels
shots for everyone and *Christ*! We must celebrate your
freedom with some bong hits and Bob Marley singing *every
little thing is gonna be all right*—and we square-danced, you
and I partners, beaming and fumbling the hooked-arm
swing and then Chris B. passed out, Tall Chris magic-
markered a penis on his heel, and all hell broke loose
between the Chrises in the dark back yard, vicious fists and
bloody lips and you and I yelling *stop, fucking stop it! Stop!*
we screamed, but then we didn't want it to stop, it was too
damn funny, and we hooted, wild in wet grass, bowing,
dancing, *do-si-doe your partner*—Yes!—*promenade home!*

# Song for a Daughter Thirty Days Clean

Star Coulbrooke

In the midst of her returning,
you can feel the spreading stillness
where anguish wracked your breast,
this moment of her spoken love
worth the twenty years it took her
to discover how you waited, why
you waited, while she moved
through life like wet cement.

Before the gray sludge hardened
into forms she could not break,
she somehow softened, became pliant,
putty in her own hands, to shape
a new world she might yet inhabit.

She widens her landscape, invites
your voice, asks you to sing her
back home. The brilliance of sunset
rings with reprieve, no hard glare
of morning clanging its gong, not yet,
just this stillness, this peace, this
brush stroke of luck. This simple,
grateful moment, holding its breath.

# November 8, 2016: A Very Nasty Day in the U.S.A.

Alison McLennan

I hauled my garbage to the curb
Nasty birds perched in a nasty tree sang and squawked
songs,
which I couldn't even understand
Because those nasty birds don't chirp English

I saw my nasty neighbor and she looked a little sad
Probably because her husband died of a nasty disease
Called cancer

I am a nasty woman
        I voted against a nasty man
Who is a broken mirror
And has no plan,
but disaster

In the evening, dogs barked
Children laughed and played their nasty games
And the nasty sky was all a fire
With sunset

# Anima Mundi

Alison McLennan

The world was already broken
The anima mundi split
When another false prophet with a gilded pompadour hit

The impudent orange archangel descended from his 747
Crowned with a halo of prosthetic hair
Righteous words shot like bullets from his rifled lips
Hand slices, smug shrugs, a twisted smile
Gestures devised to beguile

He riled the ire; ignited a fire; stoked the flames with fear,
fury, division, and hate
Humanity erased
Falling down Dante's inferno
Is this our fate?

With the demagogue's rise,
Is the Republic's demise

In the barren orchard, the executioner of trees speaks to me
He says that all his dreams have become nightmares
The empire is built on lies
We must not destroy others and the natural world,
So that we may thrive while everything around us dies

Whether tyranny triumphs, or smolders in defeat
On this election night, divided and broken
We all lose
The Opus Magnus remains unwritten

The Anima Mundi is still split


*In 2017, as democracy dies in darkness,
  My sorrow is a bottomless pit

# PoetFlow Community Poets

# Ogden Love Poem
Christina Miller

O, Ogden, you create a burn in my soul
God, I want to climb your mountains
Down the night away on your river's edge
End the night in your arms on Ben Lomond
Never let me go as we run our lives
On Ogden's wild streets

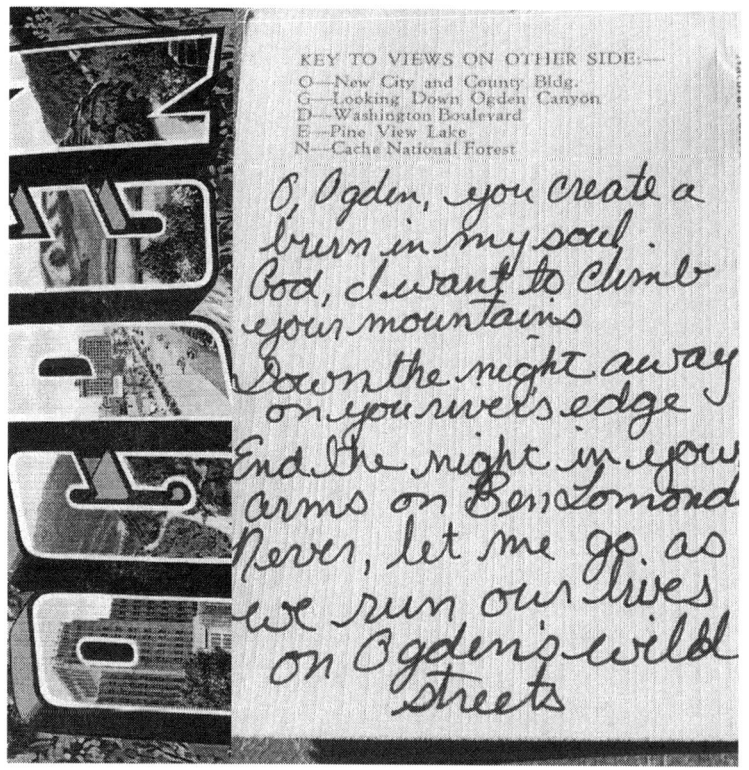

# Drive Through Memory

Christina Miller

1970s come alive – cream, brown, and a touch of orange rust.
Slight smell of musk. Brings it back to a moment, lost as the
seconds tick past each breath. Don't slip away to the dream
that was yesterday. I am home, now today!

Velvet lyrics jump from your seat yearning – the key to the
guitar case armor of my heart. The doors are open; calling
me in. Seduced by orange tones of memory.

The slow strum of each tin bead through his thumb and
index finger. "Find my love" along the chain that hangs the
song key – snap open my heart. Take the step in. Drive
through memory 'til the melody brings me home to you
again!

# Elsinore

Christina Miller


On a crisp cool night
I decided to walk about
In the arid desert land
Of peculiar rural Utah
The Big Dipper Dripped
Across the Northern Sky
Sparkles of the Milky Way
Lit up the night sky
Perfect spring night
to stretch out and
do a little soul search
under the western moon
Visited an ancient woman
who sits on the edge of Fish Lake
A Pando worshiper
through and through
She gave me the last
of her stash of peyote
to guide me through
my journey that night
The sun sets and
I begin my trip
Going down a dusty road
to a small Utah town
I know this is the place I must stop
Once I see the name drop
I pull into the gas pump
Fill up my bronco Blue
Go inside for a hot dog and Baby Ruth

My head starts to swirl and spin in store
I decide to move this adventure
Out through the door
I walk under the only street light
Behold, I meet a dinosaur
Long and green and
A stare not so mean
I wander up to bid him adieu
Hello dinosaur, my name is Elsinore
I'd love to ride you
'Til the morning blue
The mighty dino said climb aboard
I'll take you where that ford can't go
So my dinosaur stepped off the dirt
I look back to see my Bronco on a toy set
We dashed through the universe
And touched the North Star
Came back to the Solar System
To skate Saturn's rings to Mars
But I screamed as a brilliant asteroid
Careened towards me and my trusty Dino steed
Dino came to a screeching halt
Aliens blinding us with their lights
"Do you come in peace?" I ask
"Who the hell are you?
What are you doing?"
Was the response
"I am Elsinore and
this is my dinosaur!
We are on a tour of this universe"
I plead to these Alien fiends
"I'm sorry miss. I doubt that's your name"
Said the Alien wearing dark sunglasses

"Who wears dark sunglasses on Mars?"
I think as I fall deep in thought
In a creepy-crawly voice
The Alien said
"You are not Elsinore,
that is not your dinosaur."
"This is the Sinclair Gas Station
on the Main Street of Elsinore, Utah.
You are riding the store's icon green dinosaur."
Came the voice
"So step on down miss
Get into my car
We'll head to the station
To figure out who you are"
I wake in the morning
The officer comes in.
I can't hide the smile
When I see my case file:
Elsinore and her Dinosaur.

# Neon Signs

Leonides Ortiz


Strangers on the street are like neon signs ---
Bright, in my face but oddly welcoming

I'm still afraid sometimes to smile

He broke me, my endless indulgence,
That looming mountain
always in my horizon

I can't escape

My life is two rooms connected---
my freedom sealed off by an iron gate

A gate I helped build, locked,
devoid of color

I longingly stare as the strangers pass,
willing them
    to see me
    to save me

I want to be a neon sign again.

(I wrote Neon Signs for a writing exercise for The Free
Poetry Writing class at Booked on 25th. We had to walk
around 25th Street and observe and take notes. From those
observations, we all wrote a poem.)

# The Price

Leonides Ortiz

Trinkets, trinkets everywhere
not a memory in sight

I sit under my bridge at night
hoarding baubles of flashing lights

Troll, Troll, I paid my toll
some long-forgotten summer night

Now it is winter forevermore
nothing wondrous within my sight

Alone, alone, I grumble and moan
as I roam under my bridge at night

Wandering through my trinkets,
my only source of light

# Of Soul Mates and Fuck Buddies

Mary Luna

At first dripping with the sweet, syrupy high of
yet another "once in a lifetime" love,
she is deceptively pulled
into the pseudo-safety of vulnerability.
Feeling newly alive and pleasantly raw
she will reject all probabilities
and pretentiously bet her heart.

Strutting in his repetitive robe of superiority,
he will lie in wait for her first misstep-
his piety feeding off the proof of his own supposed-stability.
Doesn't he know
fear kills Love? He rejects both,
branding her "crazy."

As if her beautiful mess of soul could be reduced to just one
word!
She is not a pedantic metronome of predictability.
She has ability to fire into orgasmic, terrifying, life-affirming
chaos;
to render muscle and fascia, fearlessly, to Create.

Yet he expels his lifeless release, not into her soft, open core
but into a womb he conjures-
One not created by woman,
but barren and masculine.
It is irrelevant. There is no intention of Life.

In spite of it, he gives her nothing. Her life is offered up as a
testament
to her passion and acceptance of so many things.
For who wants a selfish lover?

He exhumes her worth only to serve as justification for
"crazy bitch!"
and, as if he had not just emptied himself into her, sneers
"what a whore."

She shamefully accepts his selfish rhythmic thrusts;
foolish in her own unrelenting need for relief.
In a dance with her mind and his body
she seeks atonement, not knowing whether from him or for
him.

She swallows, begging him to take seed in her emptiness.
He accepts what she gives,
Allowing for the consummation of body while rejecting the
soul;
for whatever it is.

And she drinks him up to her own drunkenness.

# Same City, Two Parts

Rachelle Greenwell

I.
I met you in the hallowed hallways of Ogden High
You were attracted to my bouncing pony tail
Your curly hair and turquoise pendant resting on your chest
excited me.
I summoned my courage and talked to you about a common
interest.

Later we learned we lived on the same block on Tyler
Avenue
you came to me
I was baking cookies
The sweet smell lured you in

You became my best friend
Poured me lucky charms when I was sad
We skipped school at Galaxy Diner on Harrison
50s theme fries dunked in ranch
Washed down with sugary caramel Coca-Colas.

We planned our classes together
Exiting stage right to escape
Stolen freedoms on sunny days

We would gather for lunch on marble benches outside
English hall
Or on the steps entering into the depression era, art deco
school

Once you hugged me in my backyard by the cherry tree
I entered in your arms
With the overwhelming feeling of coming home
to the place where I belonged.

We watched stars fall
our forbidden laughter entering all the parents' windows.

Years later we dressed in white and went to the Ogden
temple
We made avocado green and rust orange promises.
The promises fleeted through the sunsets.

II.

We sat In the Lighthouse Lounge
On Historic 25th Street
Cracked red vinyl sticky against my legs
25 years of watching stars fall
reduced to numbers
Meaningless words
Negotiations

My final attempt
Reaching for you
I bought you your favorite candy
In a shot
In the dark

Going home to Roy
I crushed my red lips with my fist
Where you'd teased
One last time

Behind me you flashed your brights for some reason
I didn't notice
Didn't turn around

We met there at the turn about
You claim it was funny
I found no mirth
Eyes streaming,
Heart bleeding
So fucking glad you found it funny

You are no longer the boy in turquoise pendant and white
tee
You are a ghost that roams the halls

# Tethered Heart

Rachelle Greenwell

I took the word love off the wall
It was made of metal
But I ruined it with my bare hands
Twisted each letter to and fro
Like dark hard waves
Held together by nothing.

I tried to fit the ruined word under my bed
But it was too strong
I put it in the closet
Darkness swallowed it up

But I am afraid that
As I lay in bed
It will sneak while I'm asleep

It will come crawling across the floor
Metal edges screeching against hard wood.
Climb into bed with me
Each sharp angle burrowing into my frail skin
Every morning I will tuck it back away
Into a different dark corner
It will rust over the ages eroding into each long year
But it will always find a way back to me

Eventually I'm afraid it will un-twist itself
The letters slowly curling back into the word
And it will fly back onto the white wall
Declaring itself whole again.

# Chocolate Milk

Sarah Cox

I think chocolate milk is my soulmate.
I'd rather drink it than go on a date.

It makes me feel happy and satisfies my thirst.
I think I've got the 12-year-old palate curse!

If I have the choice between chocolate milk and having sex...
Well, that may be the reason I have an angry ex.

I love it so much, Chocolate milk is always there
This is a silly poem, but Rees made me share.

# Monster in my Closet

Sarah Cox

There is a monster in my closet.
He's an annoying little fuck.
He can make something good seem like it really, really
sucks.

There is a monster in my closet
Who whispers in my ear
Maybe you should over think that, their message wasn't
clear.

There is a monster in my closet
Who puts thoughts into my mind.
He makes me question myself, am I really being kind?

There is a monster in my closet
Who makes me feel like shit.
He makes me think these thoughts in my head might
actually be legit.

There is a monster in my closet
Will he ever go away?
Unfortunately, it feels like this monster is here to stay.

There is a monster in my closet
So I try to lock the door and lose the key.
This monster in my closet is called anxiety.

# 367 Words About Only One

Brian Bernard

This isn't a love poem.

But . . . I need you.

Again, not in the hyper-sensationalized "drive to the brightest side of the wide-western sky as the sun drips UV food dye in our oceanic atmosphere, and I'd die, simply die, if I couldn't call you *mine*" kind of lie.

But I need you.

Like a C# needs its octave to expand ever vaster, beckoning, together, in expanded heavenly chorus, the overtones created by only these two notes . . .

Or gee, honey, even a G# (as long as you're on top . . .), come as my fifth and I will drink you.

Immodestly moderating my own potential addiction, but we could still pick some notes off a canopy of audio, the sweet fruits that only you and I can reach.

However . . .

G# likes some notes I don't blend with so well . . . So I swell in jealousy?

Hell no! What did I say at first?

I would never call you "mine."

Since when is possession an expression of love of any kind?

Oh, but right, this isn't a poem about that . . .

I couldn't be so selfish to cage you, pretend you don't sound also divine with any other notes . . .

Like that D# you've been eyeing. I see you. And it's ok, he's your fifth, your extra power to keep you shining extra bright for extra long.

What is love but the musical chorus of Divine blending with Divine?

Not "yours," not "mine," but what simply happens when we sing the same line.

See . . . I need you.

And other notes, too. A melody of only two rushes to old age.

Tell me about the notes you've blended with that I can't seem to, and I'll do the same.

But . . . Can you hear all the overtones when we're honest about ourselves?

Naked, vulnerable, lung-surfing hurricane power winds through our pipes as we both confidently express our truths?

Because those are only ours. God's own instruction booklet for us to get the most out of each other.

. . . I suppose this is a love poem.

Let's sing.

# Calm Yet Untamed

Brian Bernard

Cold blush, a trail painted by gold brush,
crushed musty moss, twigs and canyon gusts
thrusting out concerns, stubborn, lovelorn and heart torn
beliefs,
rusted over by calcified repetition.
Just step, and wait to wake up trusted
dead ahead: loss, lachrymal lust, wept
letting out concerns, stubborn, lovelorn and heart torn
beliefs,
bled out by the gasp then sigh repetition.
Let breathe, and let the stones stack steep,
keeping deep internal eyes, a hypnotic reaping
revealing mine, all concerns, stubborn, lovelorn and heart
torn beliefs,
steeping out, diluting in the pacing repetition.
Stuck stone loosened by sticking to gusts and moans,
that eternal Om, internal home, primed to letting go:
all these concerns, stubborn, lovelorn and heart torn beliefs.
Get lost to find myself and conjure relief,
due east, it doesn't matter – I just get to stepping.
The heart cocooned in canyons,
the eye high on the watchtower,
it's never the end – walk east, breathe and calm yourself
while all this is still untamed.

# Cosmetic

Cindy Jones

Lucky lipstick
She lisped
thickening orange
over her iambs.
The preening of plumage
a preamble to
the umbrage
of slapstick chitchat.
December's
glacial facial
still lost
in the closet.
Ostentatious sharing
of shadows.
Dowry of
gray wrens
writhing
toward free will.

# Ogden

Cindy Jones

Ogden, little rebel city with defiance in your bones.
Your brick and whiskey alleys
a union to yesterday's tempest dreams.
Born of a father who presses cities into bootstraps,
a mother who teaches, preaches conformity.
With ghost footprints of hungry soldiers
trailing your two-bit streets;
With the fate that connected the nation
still pulsing in your railway veins
you have risen, burst and broken free
spilling out into autonomy
like your rivers in the spring.

# In the Dream

Cindy Jones

In the dream I was
sitting at a broken
table
on the street,
looking at
tattoos of trees
covering my arms.
he
sat in a cast-iron chair and
asked
why I had I not
watered the
plants in the garden this year.
I looked up from my arm trees
smiled
and said
that in fact
I had.

# Up There

Kase Johnstun

You know he's brave up there in that barren tree
that Carl guy with toes and hallux around the fingerling
branch
a pink flamingo on the edge of a black marsh sky
I don't mean he's the type to save lives, no,
he runs away from things that scare him, like you or me
But you know he's brave up there in that fragile tree
that Carl guy, you know him, caesarian raw on night's
abdomen
the black branch starts to break
I'm not saying he's a hero or anything like that, no,
he'd protect himself before saving you or me
But you know he's brave up there in that scarred tree
that guy Carl who wants to be another type of bird
his friend says that we don't fly, to get down
I won't sit here and tell you he's breaking ground, no,
he's just hanging from a tree branch, different than you and
me
I wanted to say he's brave
That's what I had written
The pink flamingo, carl
The one his friend tells to get to get down
Because we're not flying birds

# Sleeping with Dead Women

Kase Johnstun

A friend of mine likes to sleep with dead women. Already dead women. It's true. He doesn't kill them or anything sick like that. And he pays good money for it too, so it's not like he's digging them out of their graves like a thief or something.

He's a card-carrying member of a club. He only has sex with dead women who said – before they died, of course – that it was okay for people with member cards to have sex with them. They signed up for it, just in case you were wondering how someone could say, "Hey, I'm dead right? Why would it matter."

He likes the cold, inanimate feel of flesh, like the rubber of one of those abdominal balls that people use in the gym, beneath him. There are far weirder things, he tells me. Some people like much weirder things, for sure. Plus, there's a lubricant, so there's no chance of injury, he mentions this to ease my worries. I'm glad he cleared that up.

He thinks that more people should do it. That it would kill the xenophobia of it all, that it would break down some barriers between the living and the dead, and maybe, just maybe, we would all live better if we weren't scared of what happens after we die.
He says he's thought a lot about it, you know, philosophically. Thinks the world would be a better place if people could check 'yes' on their driver's license to lend their post-mortem bodies to not only science but to human satiation.

He says there'd be a lot less crazies out there if people did.

# Spinning

Donna Hernandez


Spinning spinning, flying around
My hair all around me, my feet off the ground
The feeling in my heart ~ my squeals in the air
You spin me around as fast as you dare.
You let go my hand and I stumble around
Giggling beside me, we fall to the ground
"I love you daddy!" I whisper to you
"Now do it again, spin me just like you do"

Spinning spinning, flying around,
My heart skips a beat, I see you there in the crowd.
Your eyes mesmerize me, your smile draws me in
You say "Hey I'm Steve" and our story begins
You me and MaK begin to make plans
Together we explore ways to join our two clans.
Each time you touch me, each time we kiss
When you tell me you love me, my heart it just spins.

Spinning spinning, flying around,
It's time to let go ~ somewhere else I am bound
"I may not be your number one man after today
But there's a place in my heart where you will always stay
I'm proud of the woman you have become
Our dance is now over, it's no longer my turn.
I give to you Steve, my kith and my kin
Show her nothing but love, always make her heart spin"

Spinning, spinning, flying around
Heat searing through me, my face hits the ground

Plain floods my body, my legs and my face
What happened? Am I dying? My heart begins to race.
Breathing gets harder, your face looks so sad
I want to reassure you but the pain it's too bad.
Shit this is it, I'm dying I believe
I feel the warmth of your fingers as you say "Donna, just breathe"

Spinning spinning, flying around
The pain is intense now, no breath to be found
"We might need that fib" I hear a man say
"Please make it stop" I beg and I pray
A buzzing inside me begins at my toes
Goes all through my body and ends at my nose
Darkness surrounds me, with a small warming light
If I can just touch the warmness, then things'll be alright

Spinning spinning, flying around
I'm floating above the body down there on the ground
The light's getting brighter, I'm warm and fuzzy inside
The pain is intense but I no longer hide
I no longer want this, the pain is too much
A feeling of rightness, a feeling of rush
I know if I reach out, of this pain I'll be free
I stretch for the light then I hear you say "Donna, stay with me."

Spinning spinning, flying around,
I hear people screaming as I slam to the ground.
The scene keeps replaying, day or night doesn't matter
My broken bones flinch and my heart it just shatters
Then the warmth on my cheek, your breath on my skin
"You're safe now, I'm here, she won't hurt you again

Remember I love you and this time I'll swoop in
No need for you to jump, this time we will win."

Spinning spinning flying around
I can't help but think of the time on the ground
Your touch and the warmth that spread through my hand
Showed me how much you loved me, you made me
understand
You're my hero, my soulmate and I owe you my life
I'm so thankful you wanted to make me your wife
Together we are invincible, through thick and through thin
I hope you know that I love you, for making my heart spin.

# Where Are You?

Donna Hernandez

As long as I can remember, you have always been there,
Together we laughed, we cried and we faced our fears.
When filled with self-doubt you were always the one
Who'd bolster me up and these thoughts you would turn
Into positive notes, ones filled up with glee
No matter what, you were always there for me

When I moved to the States, I felt so alone
All my family and friends remained back at home
You let me weep when I wanted, you held me when I cried
You saw right through me each time that I lied
When I said I was fine and happy to be here
You'd just smile and you'd nod, then wipe away the tears

When I started to train for my first half-marathon race
I told you my plans, you looked me right in my face.
"you can do this Donna," and "I'm right there for you
Whatever makes things easier, are the things that I'll do."
It came as no surprise because of one thing I could see
No matter what, you were always there for me

Last month when I needed you, you didn't let me down
You were there in that room, but on your face was a frown.
After surgery you were there, telling me it would be okay
When you started to go, I begged you to stay.
You stayed by my side on those first few bad days
Then things seemed different, you had changed your ways

There was a distance between us, something I'd never seen

I hated you then, so I became mean.
I said you were useless, I hated you so,
I felt you backing away but I wanted you to go
I screamed and I cried and said things in haste
When you finally left bitter tears I could taste

When I look in the mirror, this face I don't recognize
There is no happiness there, and there's a dullness to my
eyes
I feel so trapped, I feel full of shame
But I made you go, there's no-one else to blame
I know that someday of this chair I'll be free
But what happens then if I still can't find me?

# I Found Myself in Ogden

Elisabeth Huber

I found myself in Ogden after a string of depression
and defeat. Thousands of miles from home,
I met a boy through the happenstance of destiny.

Months later, we sat cross legged on the upper level of
Harrison Heights apartment,
Listening to a rare thunderstorm and rain falling fast.
Our bodies cradled together through the storm,
hands intertwined, and the newness of our love
radiating off our skin and warming our souls.

We walked across the road to Weber's Campus,
lay a blanket across the manicured grass,
felt the sun soak into our skin,
and waited for the Pop's Concert to start.

We spent the summer poor and in love.
Walking down the River Parkway,
weaving in and out of crowds at the farmers market,
searching for geocaches along Harrison,
listening to music at the Amphitheater,
finding ourselves falling in love with Ogden
And with each other.

After a summer at Harrison Heights, I moved into
University Village,
and started classes at Weber.
Classes of 25 students, deep discussions,
and shared experiences.

My first love would walk down the hill from building 3 to
Elizabeth Hall.
He would sit with me in the computer lab,
our minds both busy with school work.
Stealing glances with our hearts and minds blazing.

I found myself growing up with my love.
Snuggled in my twin bed at University Village,
I told him I was ready to marry him.
"Me too," he said.

We married and moved into a brick apartment complex on
25th Street.
On Saturday mornings, he would walk over to Toppers
and we would eat breakfast under the awning at Oasis
Garden.
We would study side by side chasing success together.

A year later, he graduated from Weber, and the following
year so did I.

I walked down the marble halls of Ogden High School,
and opened my classroom door. He carried in boxes of
books.
He moves around the students' tables
Helping me find the perfect arrangement.

On difficult days, I come home and cry.
I cry for the poverty and the pain that my students face
daily.
Cry for their short-lived childhoods.

He listens and holds me.

A few times a month, I announce community events,
"Why do you love Ogden?" my students ask.
"I found myself in Ogden" is always my reply.

I found myself reading in the library, philosophizing in the
corner of a bar on 25th Street, snuggled in a chair at the
fireplace lounge at Weber, reading on the 603.

I found myself studying at University Village, meditating at
the Oasis Community Garden, shopping at Winco, and
eating at the taco stand on Washington.

I found myself falling in love again and again with a boy
who became a man while holding my hand.

# A Tasty Treat

Elisabeth Huber

On my walk home, the scent of barbecue and crockpot stew
torment my senses until I submit to the temptation of meat
fondue.
I lament that this addiction of mine must be from the deity
because my belly craves juicy meat far too frequently.

I open the freezer and assess the situation.
flanks and shanks- Enough to feed a fire station.
The meat's tightly wrapped in packages tied with string.
I take out a parcel that came from a male offspring.

I am long overdue for a delicious beef stew.
However, there's something else I want to dig into.
I tenderize the flank and rub it with spice
and sear it in a pan to eat with fried rice.

I like my meat juicy and rare
so, I take it off the stove and retreat to my lair.
The rice is delicious and the meat is a treat,
human flesh is the best cut of meat.

# Hearts Connected

Janica Johnstun

The sun is blooming in the mud
There are stars in the trees
Sunrise in my eyes
Flower blossoms upon my tongue
As my soul compels me to speak of our Love.
My heart is in the wind
And the ocean in my heart
Swaying to the beat of native drums
I am drawn by a force universal to whisper the ceremonious
beauty of
three eternal words...
"I love you."

# Dare to Embrace Your Light

Janica Johnstun

Dare to embrace your light
The constellations within your chest
The universes giving birth within your soul.
Dare to pursue that which sparkles within you
The forests of creative ideas growing lush and blossoming in
your mind
The murals of colorful dreams that meditation creates when
you dare to reach inside.
Dare to let your spirit flow wild as the wind
Dare to follow the sun
Dare to be a spark in a parched wilderness
Setting the world on fire with the intensity of YOU ablaze
Dare to dream wide awake
To breathe in new worlds of beauty in each breath
To accept into your temple only that which is pure in essence
To let infinity blossom within each magical moment
To let magic become YOU.
To let adoration as jewels sparkle in your irises when you
and your lover meet
To let your heart dance the salsa when passion plays its
rhythm and beat.
Dare to let compassion patch up any broken places in your
soul
To welcome your emotions with non-judgement
To let yourself heal and be whole.
Dare to love yourself
For when you do, you love the universe inside of you.

# The Universe is a Giant Elephant

Janica Johnstun

The universe is a giant elephant.
She ate 300 pounds of my dreams for breakfast and has yet
to majestically give them back.
My grass, my roots, my bark, my fruit
She chomped them up like treasure cake, and sang,

"The beauty in me sees the beauty in you... Namaste."

She spread wide her ears shaped like African maps and
danced a magical dance
in the rain storm of tears I cried upon her feet.
And using her trunk of a thousand stars she covered herself
with mud to protect my dreams.

She whispered to me,
"Any dream is possible when it becomes ONE with the
universe.
You cry because I have eaten your dreams but now they
exist in both of us.

"Darling, dry your eyes. You will write, dream, and love
again. I have seen in your future this truth

If in the mud, you choose to bloom,
Beauty and Love will find you."

The universe is a giant elephant.
She ate 300 pounds of my dreams for breakfast,
and has majestically given them back.

# Ogden Untamed

Jayrod Garrett

We once were the crossroads
of the west. Capitol of the Rockies:
born of locomotives and faith.

Ogden has never been a place
of judgment– in these parts we value
hearts, minds, souls for what they offer.

Union Station the nexus of the wild west
welcomed everyone. Hearts of gold,
minds of ash, souls left forsaken.

Yet as fewer trains stopped here
more we had to mine ourselves
for the resources that would let us thrive.

Of course, when you dig too deep-
the canary dies. Or in our case, our golden goose.
Union Station stood empty and with her

the wild west came to an end. We traded her
goods as long as we could. Al Capone
and brothels became gangs and meth.

And fear consumed what had only been caution
before. Now people spoke of us like a black sheep
or a redheaded stepchild. Soulless.

Businesses settled outside our borders–

money flowed from our hands to foreign pockets
as the just desserts for the sins of our city.

But our clothing doesn't define our identity–
our hair remains brown, lush with mountains
crowned with evergreens. Our skin freckled

with easygoing folk born of the earth.
Change comes slow when people fear you
but it gives you an opportunity:

To stay true to who you are. We found ourselves
in our artists, those who climbed our peaks,
chose to make homes fearlessly.

You see when you examine the heart, mind,
and soul of Ogdenites you find treasures
greater than gold, faith, or mountains–

we laid out our doormat for the west to visit.
That hospitality doesn't die easily. We integrated
ourselves to listen to jazz music. That unity

isn't threatened by rumors. We lost
our railroad, our businesses, survived
a crippling depression we earned our keep.

Today Ogden is a place where people stand
with feet firm on the ground reaching not
east, west, north, or south, but up.

We seek the stars that like us are untamed,
fearless, bold. You can reject us if you like,

the doormat remains. We will build

our art district, our farmers market,
places for our youth to explore themselves,
and resurrect our own business sector

to shore up our foundation.
From Union Station to the Egyptian Theater,
Weber State University to the Ben Lomond Hotel,

and anyone driving down 25th Street can see
We know who we are:
Unbroken, unafraid, and welcoming.

And our doormat still remains.

# Circus Ogden (Napkin Poem)

Jayrod Garrett

Oh beautiful for mountain trails
And the river that runs through.
The storytellers drinking chai
At the Merc, Grounds, and Daily Rise.
The burlesque girls balancing swords
And the chaos of our art.
Circus Ogden
This is our circus, it runs year round
You won't find lobster claw boys or three-breasted women,
except in our art.
Ring leaders abound, replacing the ringmaster except at
Belliston's.
Round these parts we collaborate not for a good show, but
community.
We are Ogden, babyface monsters
Wingless yet soaring
This is our story.

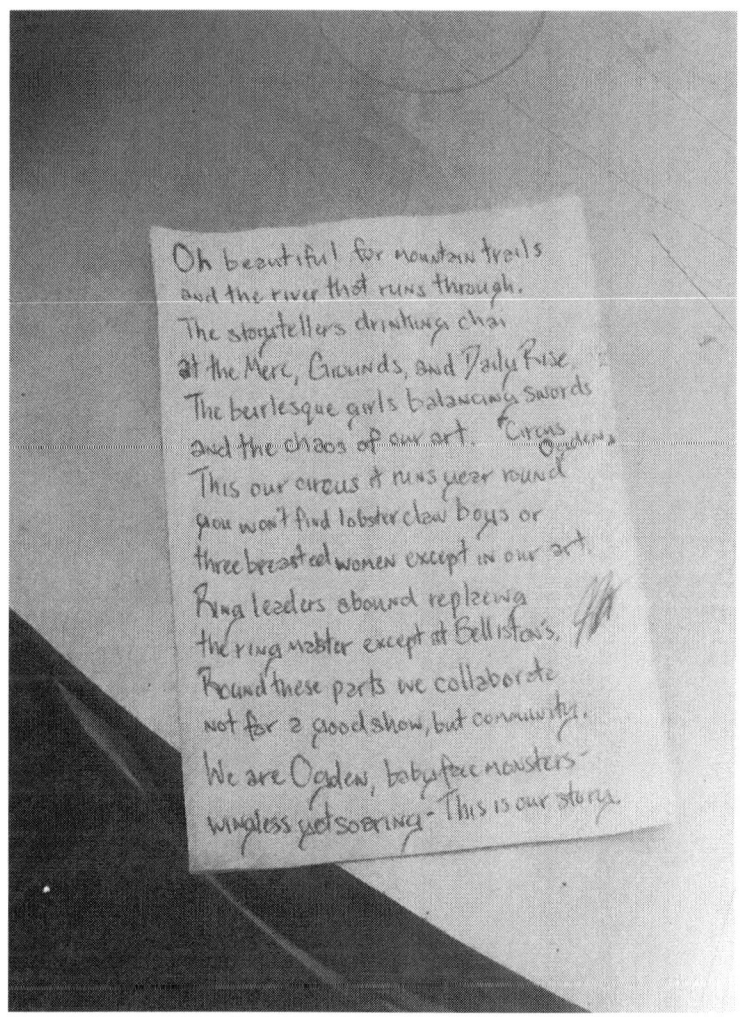

# The Legend of Jack

Jayrod Garrett

A steel locomotive runs deep
between the trees of far far away.
The hum of metal against metal
known well throughout the land
for is signified the arrival of the one
and only Jack the land had ever given
birth to. Despite so many stories
of who he was, nobody ever really
came to know Jack. But every lady
loved to see Jack come.

His legend began in the snowy
castle of the ice queen. Who thought
if she could contain his frost
she might be able to rule the winter
forever. Only Jack had other plans
as he warmed her loose caboose
leaving what was once a frozen
wasteland a wet paradise that
he warmed himself inside until
she controlled not only all things ice
but all things wet and sticky.

He left her land upon his train,
as it laid its rail through the trees.
Each rail jackhammering golden
spikes into mounds of earthy love.
As the train lurched slowly away
through twin peaks towards

the ocean the legend of Jack spread
far and wide. Even his train with
the way the earth seemed to embrace
the brutal pounding if offered her
came to be known as Jack the Ripper.

Jack be nimble and quick was known
for jumping over many candlesticks
just to please their women. To whisper in
the crook of her neck, "You are beautiful."
To leave her gasping for air,
as he left her eyes and thighs wet alike.

But Jack wasn't all about the angle cock
and blast pipe. Sometimes his train pounded
rails into the leaves of a certain beanstalk
and climbed its way up into the heavens.
Where it would promptly be chased
by a lady giant followed by her husband,
while Jack tumbled out and snuck
into the highest tower where he
and his golden woman would make music
until her harp sang Gloria to his name.

In the Christmas village one questioned
whether his name was Sprat or Horner
as he thumbed the pie of the only woman
he was known to wed. Here in this place
is where he began to spread his doctrine of
"I think I can, I think I can, I think I can,"
far and wide as one who delighted girls
with his lips and candlestick alike.

Though some screaming infidelities
approached Mrs. Horner about his
lascivious ways. They brought her his
slacks, his shirt, his underwear, and blast pipe.
Yet she'd always laugh
telling them, "You don't know Jack."
Slamming the door on their proof.
Little did they know of the truth
that she had sent him on their tracks.

Especially to the home of Peter the Piper
who put his dear sweet Pumpkin in a shell
as they rode on the Ripper. It was Jack
who rescued her leaving Peter
between cars. Far away, yet close enough
to watch as he whispered in Pumpkins ears
left her moaning and pushing him
towards her maple mound.
Wet for his tongue and happy
to please his throbbing candlestick.
Peter might have pressed charges upon
their departure, but Pumpkin taught him
to read the manual Jack left him to learn
to love her right.

For the truth was as Jack put the motion
in the locomotion of the land,
women began to stand up for themselves.
They stopped letting lovers finish first.
And pushed heads between their thighs
and giggled as they squirmed and wiggled.
And though his train visited only a few lands
domestic felicity conquered the whole world

as men began treating their women
better than their women treated them.

Mrs. Sprat one day welcomed him home
a happy grin on her face. "Leave the train
come join me on our hill like we did as kids."
Only that time when Jack fell down
and broke his ground, Jill did not come
tumbling after. Both fell in the well
and left nothing to tell, except of erotic
fairytales thereafter.

# Untitled

Kristin Thorpe

O broken Ogden
Heart of havoc
that mauled the mall
snapping its wings of cement
into soil
Craning to destroy
don't worry I won't tell your new friends
that somewhere there are good people doing bad things
that you have a huge hole in your heart at its junction
you protected yourself from company
by harboring broken wires at your core
Parents pushed their kids by hurriedly
as you lay broken for everyone to see
protect and rule your many sides
because miracle workers don't get to quit
Ogden is still untamed.

# Untitled

Kristin Thorpe

Gambling debts stacked high
he was forcing my hand
stopped by the whispers that lie in the lips of a hospital bed

He dismisses his matriarch's language as not her own
She warns me, "I am already dead"
he shakes off the curse with his head

The sadness of my doubts in her eyes
glancing at the new diamond on my finger
realizing through her own mortality
not every gangster deserves love

# Untitled #1

Billie Spears

There is a vast empty space from my eyes to your face. And I listen enough, to hear the possibilities hussshhh... silence the distance between feet and destination. How far is the walk home from your lighthouse of inspiration, to my pen writing a poem? I see the ocean space of my Everyday and the dreams that I crave. It's time to bridge the gap and start living that way, turn my mundane caterpillar existence into a butterfly poem on a page. I'm learning to hear, what you don't know how to say, with my eyes, as they clasp together lids, like hands to pray. I listen... as the voice pouring through me is that of an aged sage. We've all got sooo much to say! From the mouth of a junkie and the heart of a babe. And it's in this open valley of time I see the view from atop the cliff I've climbed. Squinting to behold how bright I shine. Though I once spent life with shut clam shell eyes, blind as a cave fish dreaming to fly. And through the rungs of that barbed wire fence of Time, I crawled out ALIVE. I ain't here to brag, don't get me wrong or pat my back. I'm just not afraid to admit, my closet of skeletons packed to the brim. I've drowned others in my efforts to swim. I've done wasted some life, I've done sinned. Yet there's a gratitude for where I've been, burns strong like a cigarette and bright like the fiery end. So... like the purest ash now, here I stand. Spit from the mouth of a junkie with so much to say (can you hear it?) And the love of a mother kneeling here to pray (can you feel it?) There it is still (can you see it?) That beautiful open space, from my eyes to your face. I want to write. A lot. But I've learned enough, to know a blank page is an alarm clock, it's time sweetheart, WAKE UP.

# Untitled #2

Billie Spears

Head north, a forested backbone highway. Wind and pine
and traffic fly by with the 13-minute drive. I crest a hill top,
snow tires almost stuck, caress the downslope with luck and
there it is... Ogden. Big brother mountain stretches arms over
its shoulders, in an eternal embrace, watching us get older.
Nestled and safe.     Ever changing and brave.
Historically insane. The boulevard like a jugular vein,
pushing the lifeblood to each avenue limb, right to the
heart... 25th Street.     Where I meet familiar faces and drink.
Where we lock lips through speech and share poetry. Where
I plant words like a tree and leave, with a new poem in utero
and waiting. Where I'm compelled to return, in snow chills
or burn. Where history and ghosts crowd each corner.
Ogden... where comfort and friendship and beauty have
truly taken form.

# Little Crumpled Wings

Patrick Ramsay

Collisions mark my windshield with delicate taps.
As if they are miniature fighter jets of a home planet
fueled by bison blood, and I am the alien mothership
invading.

The plaster of dried insides and sheen wings
sings as I fly at 1,065 miles per hour towards the island
in the sky. *Fairies*, I think to myself. Don't tell the kids
their FernGully is smeared across Uncle's car.

All for the price of a sunset, a candy-coated fix of orange
and huckleberry atop a Tuesday. Through the Causeway,
I find my usual floating spot and wait with the windows
cracked. Steadily, the mosquito riders rise.

All buzzing, all angry, looking at the genocide smeared
across the face of my '98 Suzuki. The sun leaves the room
while they tap their lances against my windows chanting,
*Murderer, murderer, murderer.*

# Nubilation of Ogden

Patrick Ramsay

There's something about a banjo
under the harvest moon.

A stage in the center of the street,
people sitting in the intersection

while traffic lights cycle —
red, green, yellow.

A city wanting to be a city,
its people objecting

with slow tapping feet,
with bobbing shoulders,

with carefully brushed hair
despite the windstorm,

with American Sign Language
insisting this Saturday be slow.

And bye, bye Miss American Pie
insisting this city remembers

how to be a town
despite the condominiums.

# Lighthouse

Rees Sweeten

light
beckons
through the mist
the waves crashing
hollers of friendship
horns blow in the distance
leading the ship to dry land
the passengers' feet touch the sand
arm and arm, embracing, they all weep
their souls saved, never again, lost at sea
— Lighthouse

# Metamorphosis

Rees Sweeten

I once had a lump in my esophagus
so large I couldn't breathe.
But I drank from the chalice of poetry,
poetry taught me to speak.
In my throat were cocooned caterpillars
yet to break free. I vocalized,
I gave these butterflies wings.

# Lost at Sea

Rees Sweeten

The sailor drifted through tides,
searched in vain, with strained eyes
To Poseidon, water god, he prayed:

*Down me in your cooling embrace*
*With mercy, succumb me in waves*
*I'm too scared to take my own life*
*Please, tip my ship, force the dive*
*I've dropped anchor, cut its line,*
*lest I taint others with dismal ties*
*I beg, take me now, end my strife*

Through fog,
he saw a high light
Things wouldn't go
as he'd thought so
on such a night
The strong ocean winds
had a plan of their own
Whistling, to the shore
his ship they'd blown

He scoffed: *The gods have a sense of humor*
*Perhaps, my wounds spirits will suture*

Feet squishing in moist sands,
he followed yellow in the sky
As his toes touched dry land
a structure beneath he'd find

He expected muskets at the door
But instead, smiles, paintings,
good people the interior adorned
He need not wander further
Warmed, he heard, a beautiful server:

*This is your first time here I'd wager*
*There's plenty of rum, plus fine beer,*
*what can I get for you stranger?*

*I will take something strong,*
*that'll put my dick in the dirt*
He said: *I've too much torment;*
*I am forever hurt*
*We have dollar drafts,*
*we have liquor* she explained:
*but those only prolong your pain*
*You're not the first to stumble in full of gloom*
*take a good look at what's in the east room*

He witnessed many take turns atop a soapbox,
from a different universe their voices did talk
Each person, a speaker, and of the crowd
He couldn't make sense of all he'd found

He protested:
*I'm no talking man, nor a bard*
*It's okay,* the server insisted:
*just speak from your heart*
*This isn't a place to drown*
*your sorrow, or your sins*
*This is a place you can say*

*all the things you never did*
*Let it out, my friend*

Burning chest,
the sailor stood up,
spoke his mind,
felt past terrors,
a force escape from each line
Never did he want to speak
of his deepest, darkest fears
But he expressed them
then, healing brought music to their ears
Unexpected, the crowd understood,
they embraced him in hugs
It was so new, so overwhelming
for the sailor, feeling loved
His legs nearly buckled,
weak at the knees
He never again
wanted to be
lost at sea.

The clouds parted,
the night no longer stormbound
The sailor wouldn't depart
A loudmouth he had found
A weekly home called
The Lighthouse Lounge

# 25 Summers

Tanner Lee

Every day in July I walked on top of trains
standing on the steel that brought fire to Zion

tonight I want to throw myself backwards
book a stay at the Rose Room

with a hooker named Rapture
(because she'll take you to heaven)

rattle chips and speakeasies
too wild for Al Capone

wander the understreets
adorned with shadows and bones

move hooch with bootleggers
brawl outside KoKoMo.

This summer,
history swallows its tantrum

we are blank slates
two kids with crayons and a white wall

the three-block city swells,
edges of the sky fold outward

stars appear like white freckles.
We paddle through the night

to the beat of hymns
swallowing the air like clumsy birds

# Minivan

Tanner Lee

he rolls me out like Friday morning trash.
the back seat smells like milk.
sprinkler water pecks the glass.

tonight we'll earn our admission to hell.

snap back elastic
bra straps over socks
my head rests on bundled jeans.

he is red and newly grown.

i learn a new use for my hands. he
asks new things of my body.

he runs down my shins like a shotgun barrel
our stomachs clap
with the wet slap of adolescence.

we're alive, that's crazy enough.

a fly struggles in the window.
trapped in the glass.

i reach over
and let
him out.

# About the Poets

Brad L. Roghaar is Faculty Emeritus at Weber State University where he taught literature and creative writing for over 30 years. He is former Editor of Weber Studies: the contemporary west. Brad's poetry has appeared in many journals and magazines. His first book, *Unraveling the Knot: Poems of Connection*, won the Pearle M. Olsen award, and he was named Utah Poet of the Year. A popular reader and presenter, Brad currently serves as Ogden, Utah's first Poet Laureate.

Shannielle Faith is a spoken word poet who uses writing as a tool to heal others. She has represented Utah at the Women of the World Poetry Slam for three years and made Salt Lake's national team in 2017. When she's not writing, she's working as a substance use counselor.

Shanan Ballam is the author of the poetry chapbook *The Red Riding Hood Papers* (Finishing Line Press 2010) and the full-length poetry collection *Pretty Marrow* (Negative Capability Press 2013). She teaches poetry writing, fiction writing, and academic writing at Utah State University.

Star Coulbrooke, Poet Laureate of Logan City, Utah, is co-founder and coordinator of Helicon West, a bi-monthly open readings/featured readers series. Published in lit mags and anthologies, her poems are also available in chapbooks, notably *Thin Spines of Memory* and *Walking the Bear*. (*WTB* is available through the Digital Stacks at the University of Utah Marriott Library.) Star is director of the Utah State University Writing Center.

Alison McLennan, MFA, co-created the Ogden Inspired Writing Series. Her first novel, *Falling for Johnny*, won an honorable mention in the 2012 Utah Original Writing Competition and the 2013 Inkubate Blockbuster Challenge. Locally set, *Ophelia's War: The Secret Story of a Mormon Turned Madam*, was published by Gale-Cengage in 2016.

Janica Johnstun: "I believe in loving bravely."

Christina Miller is a local creative whose preferred mediums are poetry and photography. She loves all things Ogden, and you'll see her supporting most Ogden art events. Christina has been a part of PoetFlow since the first gathering in September 2015.

Leonides Ortiz: Born and raised in Rochester, NY. I moved to Utah almost two years ago for grad school. I want to be a librarian who writes poetry and tells wacky stories. I truly believe the way to save us is to connect us and poetry and storytelling do exactly that.

Mary Luna: Mary most relates to Alice in Wonderland who said, "I knew who I was this morning, but I've changed a few times since then." As such, she may be anywhere doing anything, or nowhere doing nothing; but never nowhere doing anything nor anywhere doing nothing. After all, we're not all mad here!

Rachelle Greenwell: A lover of unicorns, rainbows, and wine, Shell lives life to the fullest. She regularly attends PoetFlow to share her spirit through her words.

Sarah Cox: Sarah is a mom, speech language pathologist, photographer, and lover of all things Ogden. She began going to PoetFlow to support a friend and quickly became drawn into the cathartic act of bringing words to the page.

Brian Bernard: If a situation is too hot to handle, I remember that as a dragon and alchemist, I can use that heat as leverage for my evolution. Art, music, wine and coffee connoisseur born and raised in Utah, discovering living on and with purpose in Seattle.

Cindy Jones has been churning out stories in her head since the age of 11, when she got in trouble with her 6th grade teacher for creating fictional journal entries. As a mom, wife, freelance writer, book-marketer and aspiring photographer, Cindy considers herself a noticer, pulling metaphor and seeking ordinary miracles from the everyday human experience.

Kase Johnstun is the author of *Beyond the Grip of Craniosynostosis* (McFarland & Co, 2015), and winner of the 2015 Gold Quill, League of Utah Writers. He was also co-author and editor for *Utah Reflections: Stories from the Wasatch Front* (History Press, 2014). He served on the editorial board for Label Me Latina/o Literary Journal, Queens University, Charlotte. He also serves as Literary Chair for the Ogden City Arts Advisory Committee.

Donna Hernandez is originally from Scotland but now lives in Ogden. She loves the eclectic culture of Ogden and is in awe of the amazing artists found here. She bleeds purple (Go Wildcats!). She is not an artist but uses writing as her own form of therapy.

Elisabeth Huber has lived in Ogden since 2013. She quickly fell in love with Weber State and the community. She teaches English at Ogden High School.

Jayrod Garrett is a local artist of many varieties in Ogden, known for sharing his often raw and unfiltered poetry, and for stirring performances on stage. He has also presented his poetry with Moments on 25th Street in Ogden. Most days, if you catch him, he is involved with a project called "Napkin Poetry." If you ask, he'll make you a napkin poem. Promise!

Kristin Thorpe primarily writes science fiction short stories, and is presently also working on a science fiction novel. She has a bachelor's degree in Philosophy from the University of Utah, and specialized in the philosophy of ethics. Kristin grew up in Ogden but presently lives in Salt Lake, where she is the founder/organizer of Just Write Salt Lake City, a writing group with 1,500+ writers.

Billie Spears traveled in mountains dark, sad, dreary, 'til truth came cracking booming thru. She searched never-ending for you sweet love family, you appeared thankfully glory full moon. Now she fills the room with spark joy laughter, and her heart carries the eternal peaceful tune.

Patrick Ramsay is a queer writer who was raised in a Mormon military family in Northern Utah. He earned a BA in English with a creative writing emphasis from Weber State University, where he served as editor-in-chief of the undergraduate literary journal *Metaphor*.

Rees Sweeten started writing poetry after he attended PoetFlow's weekly open mic. He attained catharsis through spoken word, composing hundreds of poems in one year, discovering love and identity in his journey. The intense introspection in Rees's poetry asks us all what it means to be a human being.

Tanner Lee lives in Ogden, Utah, and studies at Weber State University. His writing has appeared in Hobart, Glass, and Lost Sparrow Press, and is forthcoming in The Comstock Review, Clementine Unbound, and The Gambler. He is an assistant blog manager at The Blueshift Journal. Find him on Twitter @heytannerlee.

# About the Publisher

Glass Spider Publishing is a hybrid micropublisher located in Ogden, Utah. The company was founded in 2016 by writer Vince Font to bring light to the work of underrepresented authors. Visit www.glassspiderpublishing.com to learn more.

66904189R00064

Made in the USA
Middletown, DE
09 September 2019